IS PRESIDENT TRUMP FACING AN INDICTMENT ?

Exploring the Legal Implications of a Possible Indictment

Ken Myers

Table of contents

CHAPTER ONE

CHAPTER TWO

CHAPTER THREE

CHAPTER FOUR

CHAPTER ONE

Five important takeaways from the news about the Trump indictment

The former president of the United States, Donald Trump, has been charged by a grand jury in New York with covering up money paid to adult film actress Stormy Daniels.

The office of District Attorney Alvin Bragg stated that it had gotten in touch with Trump's lawyer "to coordinate his surrender" for an arraignment.

The excellent jury's prosecution and Best's charges stay under seal, and NPR hasn't had the option to affirm different media reports that the DA might summon Trump on Tuesday.

The most recent news-related information can be found here.

1. For several months, the grand jury has been looking into Trump.

According to Kim Wehle, a former U.S. attorney who is now a law professor at the University of Baltimore, Trump is likely to be charged with violating New York penal code 175.10, which entails falsifying business records in the first degree. Trump has been indicted by a grand jury in Manhattan.

Wehle told Adrian Florido of NPR's All Things Considered, "It's quite serious, even if the charge itself doesn't reach the heights that some people would expect from a former president."

Michael Cohen, Trump's former attorney, made a deal with porn star Stormy Daniels in which he paid her $130,000 in return for her silence regarding an alleged affair with Trump.

That money was sent to Daniels by Cohen less than two weeks before the election. Following Trump's victory, he paid back Cohen, including with his own personal checks. Despite admitting that he reimbursed Cohen for money paid to Daniels, Trump has denied having an affair with her.

It is incorrectly stated by the Trump Organization that those reimbursement payments were for legal fees. According to Wehle, that is a felony in New York if it was done to cover up another crime, likely the violation of campaign finance laws, in this case.

According to Wehle, a conviction for falsifying business records could result in a four-year prison sentence because it is a Class E felony.

2. Trump was requested to surrender, but it is unknown whether he will.

Previous President Donald Trump's confidential plane, known as Trump Power One, stopped on the landing area at the Palm Oceanside Global Air terminal on Tuesday in Florida.

Thursday evening, a statement from Bragg's office stated that the office had contacted Trump's attorney to "coordinate his surrender."

The spokesperson added, "Guidance will be provided when the arraignment date is selected."

Whether Trump is still in Florida cannot be independently verified by NPR. Since the 757 flew to West Palm Beach five days ago, no movement on his private plane was detected by two reliable flight trackers.

However, Florida Gov. Ron DeSantis, a Republican, stated on Twitter following the announcement of the DA's request for Trump's surrender that his state would not assist in the arrest and extradition of the former president in the event that this situation arose.

The rule of law is undermined when the legal system is used as a weapon to advance political goals.

It's not American.

The Manhattan District Attorney, who receives funding from George

Soros, has a history of bending the law to excuse criminal conduct and downgrade felonies. He is now, though.

DeSantis is widely considered to be a leading Republican presidential contender in 2024 and a threat to Trump's reelection campaign, despite the fact that he has yet to declare his candidacy.

DeSantis stated to reporters earlier this month that he would not participate "in any way" in the spectacle.

According to a report from POLITICO, he said, "I have no interest in getting involved in some type of manufactured circus by some Soros DA," referring to the campaign contributions made by billionaire donor George Soros. He is attempting to stage a political spectacle, but I have real problems in the state of Florida that I must address.

3. The indictment, according to Trump and the GOP, is political persecution.

In a statement released on Thursday, the former president

characterized the vote of the Manhattan grand jury to indict him as "political persecution" and "election interference."

According to the statement that can be found on his website, "The Democrats have lied, cheated, and stolen in their obsession with trying to 'Get Trump,' but now they've done the unthinkable, indicting a completely innocent person in an act of blatant Election Interference."

Republicans broadly echoed this sentiment, bolstering Trump's narrative of political martyrdom during the campaign.

Bragg has "irreparably damaged our country in an attempt to interfere in our Presidential election," House Speaker Kevin McCarthy wrote on Twitter. Ronna McDaniel, Chairwoman of the Republican National Committee, described the investigation as a "blatant abuse of power from a DA focused on political vengeance."

Don't refer to them as "witch hunts." The majority of Americans believe that the Trump investigation is fair. House Judiciary Chair Jim

Jordan, R-Ohio, made a one-word statement: " Outrageous."

Jordan, along with House Oversight Committee Chair Jim Comer, R-Ky., earlier this month, and the Republican Chair of the House Administration Committee, Bryan Steil, sent a letter to Bragg requesting the former president's investigation-related documents, communications, and testimony.

In response, Republican requests for its documents and testimony were described as "an unprecedented inquiry into a pending local prosecution" by Bragg's office.

4. **Accountability, according to Democrats and those associated with the investigation.**

Democrats also embraced a party message that stressed the need for blind justice, best exemplified by the expression "no one is above the law."

Former Democratic House Speaker Nancy Pelosi stated, "No one is above the law, and everyone has the right to a trial to prove their innocence."

The facts and the law have been considered by the Grand Jury.

Everyone is entitled to a trial to establish their innocence, and no one is above the law.

It is hoped that the former president will peacefully respect the system that bestows that right on him.

"A country of regulations should consider the rich and strong responsible, in any event, when they hold high office. Particularly when they do," said Rep. Adam Schiff, D-Calif., a former manager of impeachment.

The indictment also demonstrates that "no one is above the law," according to Trump's former lawyer and key witness, Michael Cohen. However, he took the opportunity to request that the matter be decided in court.

Cohen stated, "It is better for the case to let the indictment speak for itself now that the charges have been filed." I want to say two things right now: "Accountability is important, and I stand by my testimony and the evidence I gave to [the New York district attorney]."

The adult film star's attorney, Clark Brewster, commented on the indictment via Twitter, stating that it "is no cause for joy."

He tweeted, "The conscientiousness and hard work of the grand jurors must be respected." Now, let justice and truth prevail."

Daniels herself offered two responses: " Many thanks."

5. This could be only the start of Trump's legitimate hardships.

Not just Stormy Daniels is involved. In light of the rapidity and significance of this news cycle, it is important to keep in mind that Trump is also under scrutiny in other investigations that could result in their own charges.

The pressure campaign Trump and his allies used in the weeks following the 2020 presidential election is the focus of a case in Fulton County, Georgia.

For the purpose of conducting an investigation into Trump's role in starting the Jan. 6 attack, the Justice Department has questioned a number of Trump allies and aides.

Additionally, the Justice Department has initiated a second investigation into Trump as a result of a cache of classified documents.

When these probes, if any, would result in charges is unknown.

CHAPTER TWO

Investors are betting that criminal charges will actually assist the former president and make him richer, as Trump's SPAC surges 10% on the indictment, implying a $100 million gain for Trump

Between Thursday night's market close and Friday morning, shares of a special purpose acquisition company associated with Trump surged by approximately 10%.

Investors cannot directly purchase shares of Trump's company, which remains private, but they can purchase stock in the publicly traded SPAC, which would give them a share of Trump's business if the entities complete their merger. The former president's Trump Media and Technology Group owns Truth Social, a Twitter knockoff.

Investors might bet that Trump's Truth Social, where he now posts the same all-caps, misspelled messages that made his Twitter feed famous, will be the focus of criminal charges. "THIS IS AN ATTACK ON OUR COUNTRY THE LIKES OF WHICH HAS NEVER BEEN SEEN BEFORE," he wrote on Thursday night. "These Thugs and Radical

Left Monsters have justjust +2.1% INDICATED the 45th President of the United States of America."

That kind of thing could theoretically draw in a crowd, which would increase advertising revenue and benefit Trump's business. However, the preliminary data suggest that outcomes may not conform to investors' expectations. Trump's Reality Social record recorded 5.05 million supporters on Friday morning, up just a hair from 5.04 million two days sooner.

The former president is the only person with a greater stake in this situation. According to filings with the Securities and Exchange Commission, Trump holds 73.3 million shares of the merged entity. Investors were expressing the belief that Trump's stake was worth approximately $957 million when the markets closed on Thursday night, when shares were trading at $13.06. The market was suggesting that Trump's stake was worth approximately $1.057 billion by Friday morning, when shares traded for $14.42.

Trump might get even more out of the excitement. If the price of the merged company stays above $15 for some time, the merger agreement stipulates that Trump and the other shareholders of his company will receive bonus shares. Trump would gain an estimated 12.8 million additional shares as a result, totaling $192 million at $15 per share.

But before Trump could get his hands on all of that cash, a lot of things would have to happen. The merger of Digital World and the Trump Media and Technology Group is far from certain. The venture is being investigated by the SEC, Department of Justice, and Financial Industry Regulatory

Authority, who are looking into things like trading activity and communications between Trump's business and the SPAC. Digital World has already three times extended the date by which it plans to merge while the authorities are working on it. Two weeks ago, it also fired its CEO.

The company's stock could easily plummet following the merger, even if it were to occur. Computerized World stock has previously tumbled from a high of $175 to its current $14.42. Shares briefly rose during previous news events, such as when Trump hinted at running for president in 2024, before declining once more.

Additionally to be considered: the possibility of Trump being found guilty. How exactly that might affect his relationship with the social media company is still unknown. In the event of a "material disruptive event," Digital World and the Trump Media and Technology Group's merger agreement stipulated that the former president's ownership and role in the company would be structured to ensure continuity. That was one of two things it defined as such: either Trump announcing a new political campaign or the former president personally being found guilty of a crime.

The first has proactively occurred. The second might also now.

CHAPTER THREE

The New York grand jury indicted Trump on approximately 30 counts

The specific charges are still sealed, but they are expected to be made public during Trump's arraignment on Tuesday. After the indictment, the attorney asserts that Trump "will not take a plea deal."

After he was indicted on Thursday, two people who are familiar with the situation informed NBC News that former President Donald

Trump is facing approximately 30 charges of document fraud in New York City. These charges are connected to hush money that he allegedly paid to cover up his affairs.

The specific charges are obscure in light of the fact that the prosecution stays under seal until Trump who is battling to recover the administration in 2024 is supposed to show up in court for his arraignment Tuesday, however Manhattan Lead prosecutor Alvin Bragg could uncover them sooner.

The case is just one of at least three criminal investigations into Trump, who is also the only president of the United States to have been impeached twice in one term.

Dave Aronberg, the prosecutor in Palm Beach County, Florida, where Trump lives, stated on Friday on MSNBC, "Although Alvin Bragg is the first prosecutor in the history of our country to indict a former president, he's likely not going to be the last."

Trump likewise faces both government and state examinations concerning his endeavors to upset the 2020 political decision, which have been getting some decent forward momentum. Additionally, the federal special counsel is looking into Trump's involvement in the discovery of hundreds of classified documents at his private club and home in Florida.

The case in New York City centers on more than a quarter of a million dollars paid to two women before the 2016 election, including adult film star Stormy Daniels, to keep quiet about alleged affairs Trump had with them. Prosecutors are expected to claim that Trump tried to cover up these alleged affairs illegally.

Prosecutors likely filed separate charges for each payment in question, which resulted in the large number of allegations.

While Trump has denied the affair, the payments have been acknowledged.

According to two people with knowledge of the Manhattan grand jury's work, prosecutors also questioned witnesses about an earlier alleged hush money payment to Karen McDougal, a former Playboy playmate.

According to court documents, longtime former Trump attorney Michael Cohen pleaded guilty in 2018 to violating campaign finance laws and admitted to making $130,000 and $150,000 in hush money payments to two women "at the direction of a candidate for federal office," a clear reference to Trump, though he was not named "with the purpose of influencing the [2016] election."

The sums match what Daniels and McDougal were paid.

Trump has denied McDougal's claim that she had an affair with him for months shortly after he married Melania Trump. In a "catch-and-kill" effort to safeguard Trump, she was compensated through the parent company of the National Enquirer, a Trump-aligned tabloid that acquired exclusive rights to her story but never published.

The government's most prominent witness is now Cohen. Prosecutors are likely to make the claim that Trump hid payments to Daniels and McDougal that amounted to illegal campaign expenditures by falsifying business records.

Trump is likely to be charged by prosecutors with falsifying business records, which is a crime that becomes a felony when the false records are used to cover up another crime, like campaign finance violations in this case.

Trump has asserted that the prosecution is a political witch hunt and that the payments were a legal expense.

Trump wrote on his Truth Social platform on Friday, "The Judge "assigned" to my Witch Hunt Case, a "Case" that has NEVER BEEN CHARGED BEFORE, HATES ME."

In an interview with NBC's "Today" show on Friday, Trump attorney Joe Tacopina stated that there is "zero chance" the former president will accept a plea deal. He also insisted that Trump anticipates being vindicated either prior to or during a trial.

"In this case, President Trump will not accept a plea deal. "It won't happen," Tacopina declared. There is no offense. I couldn't say whether it will come to preliminary since we have significant lawful difficulties."

The New York Police Department (NYPD) has instructed its entire uniformed force to prepare for deployment in the event of unrest on Friday, as some Trump supporters have called for protests. Security is extremely tight around the lower Manhattan courthouse.

Keechant Sewell, the city's police commissioner, stated that "the NYPD always remains prepared to respond" and that "there are no credible threats to the city at this time."

Republicans, including those who hope to defeat Trump in 2024, came together in support of the former president and pledged to investigate and protest the Manhattan D.A. 's indictment, which they claim is motivated by politics.

Experts point out that the Manhattan D.A. regularly brings such cases, despite Trump and his allies' assertions that he is being singled out for charges that are rarely brought by prosecutors.

However, the Manhattan District Attorney's office has previously decided not to press charges against Trump due to the fact that numerous legal experts have questioned whether Trump would be subject to felony charges. Bragg may have additional evidence to support the case.

CHAPTER FOUR

Congress leaves before the indictment of Trump

House Majority Leader Steve Scalise (R-LA) arrives for a press conference on March 28, 2023, in Washington, DC, following a House Republican meeting at the U.S. Capitol. The Republicans got together to talk about their new energy plan, which would make energy production in the United

States easier and make environmental reviews of energy and mining projects easier.

When Trump was indicted on Thursday, lawmakers had already left for recess, but House Majority Leader Steve Scalise tweeted that the indictment was "outrageous."

In some ways, the historic indictment of former President Donald Trump last night excused Congress. Legislators from both parties benefited from the indictment's timing on Thursday evening because they had already left the Capitol hours earlier to begin the two-week Easter and Passover break.

Yes, shortly after the news broke, the carefully prepared official statements began to flow. However, lawmakers from both parties left Washington before they could respond to the constant stream of questions about Trump.

After the indictment was approved by the grand jury on Thursday afternoon, Republicans vented their fury at Alvin Bragg, the Manhattan District Attorney.

GOP backs Trump and criticizes Brag:

Sen. Chuck Grassley (R–Iowa) tweeted, "Bragg downgrades NYC felonies to misdemeanors and when it comes to indicting Pres Trump Bragg upgrades a misdemeanor to a felony."

The facts had already been examined by the Department of Justice, which concluded that there was no case against President Trump. This is the same District Attorney who has a reputation for letting violent criminals off the hook in Manhattan, but he has been laser-focused on pursuing a politically motivated prosecution of a former President. In a statement, Sen. Thom Tillis (R–N.C.) said.

Kevin McCarthy, R-Calif., is the speaker. but stated that the House would "hold Alvin Bragg and his unprecedented abuse of power to account" and that Bragg "has irreparably damaged our country in an attempt to interfere in our Presidential election." made no promises of specific action.

Ky. senator Rand Paul appeared to offer Bragg a wish list, mentioning the fate of another DA: I'm curious to know if DA Bragg remembers Durham DA Mike Nifong, who withheld exculpatory DNA tests from the Duke lacrosse players. He was along these lines constrained out of office, disbarred, and indicted for disdain of court."

Olivia and Burgess conducted interviews with more than 40 Republicans on Capitol Hill prior to the indictment, including 32 Freedom Caucus members. The results showed that, despite new polling showing that Trump is expanding his lead in the primary, Trump's once-fervent supporters are now keeping quiet about whether they will support him for the GOP presidential nomination in 2024.

Will the indictment on Thursday unite the GOP behind its leader? That is yet to be determined. However, even though his challengers have largely not yet begun to intensify their outreach to Capitol Hill, the former president's influence over Hill Republicans was decreasing.

Dems respond:

"Mr. Trump is governed by the same laws as every other American.

According to a statement released on Thursday night, Senate Majority Leader Chuck Schumer (D–N.Y.), "He will be able to avail himself of the legal system and a jury, not politics, to determine his fate according to the facts and the law," Schumer said.

The grand jury has acted in accordance with the law and the facts. Everyone is entitled to a trial to establish their innocence, and no one is above the law. Former Speaker Nancy Pelosi (D–Calif.) stated, "I hope the former president will peacefully respect the system, which grants him that right."

In the meantime, Sen. Brian Schatz (D–Hawaii) does not require your or anyone else's preconceived ideas: He tweeted, "Just a reminder that there is no requirement that you express your opinion prior to reading the indictment."